Dear Nobody...

Dear Aunty...

written by

Patricia Borlenghi

Consultant:
Dr. Mahnaz Hashmi

This book has been approved by ChildLine

BLOOMSBURY
CHILDREN'S
BOOKS

For Lara

First published in Great Britain in 2001
Bloomsbury Publishing Plc, 38 Soho Square, London, W1V 5DF

Copyright © Patricia Borlenghi 2001

The moral right of the author has been asserted
A CIP catalogue record of this book is available
from the British Library

ISBN 0 7475 4735 1

Printed in Great Britain by Clays Ltd, St Ives plc

10 9 8 7 6 5 4 3 2

Contents

Introduction   7

School   9

Friends   18

Families   27

Growing Up   38

Body Changes   47

Periods   57

Appearance   67

Health Issues   78

Emotions   87

Secret Worries   92

Boys   105

Sex   111

Helplines   119

Educational Information   124

Websites – General Information   126

Introduction

Growing up, families, problems with friends, boys or teachers – all these issues have particular dilemmas associated with them – dilemmas that we all share. But who can you go to for advice? Often it is difficult to talk to your parents or a teacher or even your friends, especially if they are involved. Who can you rely on for advice and be certain they won't tell your secrets? Who will respect your worries and know how to direct you to find a solution? You need look no further than this informative and reassuring book for the answers to all your questions, however big or small.

Arranged under headings such as School, Friends, Body Changes and, of course, Boys and Sex, the helpful advice given by Aunty will help put your mind at rest. The book contains letters from girls everywhere, girls just like you who are coming to terms with lots of complicated things, like changing relationships and growing up. And remember that your problems are the same as those experienced by girls everywhere, so although you are unique, you are not alone! The letters here prove just that. But if you still need answers please refer to the back of the book where you will find a long list of addresses and websites specially selected for you to contact for further information.

School

Dear Aunty

The girls in my class pick on me *because* I always know the answers to the questions teachers ask, and I always come top in end-of-term exams. When my friend and I are in the playground some girls even throw things at us. My friend is being bullied just because she hangs round with me. I've always *been* able to handle this up until now, *but* I just can't take any more and I don't know what to do about it.

Minnia, aged 11

Dear Minnia

However difficult it may seem, you should try to talk to an adult about this – a teacher you trust, or your parents. They need to know what's going on at school. Maybe your parents and the headteacher can meet together and try to solve this problem.

Bullying can destroy your self-confidence and make you dread going to school. It might be a good idea to keep a record of the bullying and get your friend to do the same. Some schools have councils, which act like a forum or group meetings where human rights and issues such as bullying, race and homosexuality are addressed. If your school has such a council, you could arrange to bring this issue up. If your school hasn't got a council, then you could certainly try and set one up. One of your teachers will be able to help you.

For more advice on bullying, see the back of the book.

Best wishes   *Aunty*

☆ ☆ ☆ ☆ ☆

Dear Aunty

I am 14 and have missed quite a lot of school because I broke my leg in several places in a skiing accident. I have had two operations and was on crutches for a long time. I am nearly at the end of my first year of studying for my GCSEs and I am really worried about how much work I have missed. How will I ever be able to catch up?

Tina, aged 14

Dear Tina

Sorry to hear about your broken leg. It must have been very disruptive for you, at home as well as at school. You should try to discuss your worries about catching up with your parents and class teacher. It might be possible for you to have some extra tuition either through the school, or if not, your parents might be able to arrange for you to have a private tutor to cover the areas where you feel you need help. Alternatively there are lots of GCSE study guides available either at bookshops or on the Internet. See the back of the book for more information.

Best wishes   Aunty

Dear Aunty

I will be taking 10 GCSEs in the summer and
am not that confident of passing them all.
There is a lot of pressure on me to do well in
my grades but sometimes I really think I am
not coping at all well with the pressure of it all.
Why are exams so important?

Sophie, aged 15

Dear Sophie

I am afraid exams are important because our
society still judges people by how many exams
they have passed. There is a lot of pressure on
girls about to take their exams. This is partly to
do with parental expectation. Most parents
want their children to do well in exams; they
want the best for you and want you to get a
good job. But you must try not to worry unduly
about exams. They are part of going to school. If
you do have anxieties, try to talk to someone
about it. Your parents or your class teacher may
help. However, some of the most supportive

people can be friends who are going through the same experience. If you have an older brother or sister, they might be sympathetic about what you are going through, and help you talk about it. The more worried you are, the more likely you are to be tense about taking your exams. Just try to enjoy the subjects you like best as much as you can, and if you need help with any others, there are lots of study guides available on the market. Your teacher will be able to recommend some to you, and see the information at the back of the book.

Best wishes *Aunty*

☆ ☆ ☆ ☆ ☆

Dear Aunty

My maths teacher always seems to be picking on me, and I get so nervous I can never answer any of her questions. Help!

Lindsey, aged 12

Dear Lindsey

Are you sure it's only you she's picking on? Have a word with your classmates. Do they feel picked on too? It might just be the style of her teaching. Try to make an extra effort to read up on maths before each lesson – you might even dazzle her with your amazing answers. But if you really do think there is a problem, have a word with your maths teacher to see what she has to say. If you can't face doing that, speak to your class teacher or a teacher you trust and see if there is any solution.

Best wishes   *Aunty*

☆ ☆ ☆ ☆ ☆

Dear Aunty

I am very short sighted and have to wear thick glasses. Lots of girls at school call me 'specky', 'four-eyes', or 'goggle-eyes'. Sometimes I can't face going to school. What can I do?

Gloria, aged 13

Dear Gloria

Classmates can be cruel and spiteful. If you have the courage, put your chin up in the air and tell them glasses are groovy! Refuse to talk to them if they persevere in their name-calling. Once they realise that they can't get to you, they'll stop teasing you. It is best to tough this kind of thing out.

Most people wear glasses at some point in their lives. In fact some people think glasses are positively sexy, what about Mel B for an example? They can even be a fashion accessory or fashion statement, and some people who don't even need glasses wear them! Maybe you could talk to your parents about getting some special thin lenses for your glasses, and perhaps you might even be ready to start wearing contact lenses at some stage. You can also arrange to make an appointment with your optician to discuss all the various options.

Best wishes  Aunty

Dear Aunty

All my friends tease me and say I have a crush on my history teacher. He is my favourite teacher, and I do like him a lot but how can I stop these rumours from spreading? I would hate him to hear about it.

Meera, aged 13

Dear Meera

Don't worry about this too much. All girls have crushes on teachers – male and female. It's just a stage you go through, when you have a need for someone or something to be the object of your affections, or when you need to idolise somebody who is much older than you. It's all perfectly natural. When your friends tease you, either ignore them, or laugh about it. You can joke that 'yes' you did have a crush on him, but now you are far too mature for that kind of thing, and besides, what about the age difference? And don't worry if he hears about it, all teachers are used to this kind of thing.

As you get older, you will learn that nobody's perfect, even the people you idolise, and you may begin to like people the same age as you.

Best wishes   *Aunty*

Friends

Dear Aunty

My best friend and I are very close and we are always holding arms or hugging. Some girls in our class call us 'lezzies' or 'gay' and I don't know what to do about it.

Carrie, aged 13

Dear Carrie

It's great that you and your friend are so close. Try to ignore your classmates. A lot of girls and boys at school are going round these days using words like 'lezzie' or 'gay' without realising they are being very hurtful. They don't necessarily realise that they are being homophobic, which means having a fear of gays and lesbians. They use these terms for all kinds of things, without meaning any real harm, but they have to be educated to realise that this kind of name-calling is wrong. It can lead to bullying and all sorts of problems for the person who has been labelled in this way. If you have a school council, this is the kind of thing you could bring up.

Your friends are being immature and igno-rant. There is nothing wrong with being close to another girl. It's good to show your feelings and be affectionate. However, it may be an idea to reduce your displays of affection in front of certain people in some situations.

Best wishes *Aunty*

☆ ☆ ☆ ☆ ☆

Dear Aunty

I have a friend who is stealing things from other girls at school. I have seen her with sweets, pens and money that I know do not belong to her. What can I do?

Penny, aged 12

Dear Penny

This is a very serious situation. Your friend is most probably seeking attention, and this is a cry for help. Maybe she has serious problems at home. She certainly needs help before the problem gets even more serious.

You could try to talk to your friend about it. She may get very angry with you and try to deny it. You have to broach the subject very gently, and try to convince her that sooner or later she will be caught, and she will be in very deep trouble which could lead to her being expelled from school, or even having the police involved.

If that doesn't work, you may need to talk to your class teacher. Hopefully the school will be sympathetic towards your friend as she has a very worrying problem. If it can be stopped now, she will be much better off, and it might help clear up any underlying problems she may have.

Best wishes   *Aunty*

Dear Aunty

I have fallen out with my two best friends.
When we go out they always seem to pair up
and I feel like the odd one out. One of them
called me selfish, and I am really fed up with
both of them.

Cindy, aged 14

Dear Cindy

It is difficult when there are three best friends
in a group. Yet your two friends can't always
pair up or they wouldn't want to go out with
you at any time, would they? Call them both
together, or try to talk to them individually
about how you feel, and try to thrash it out. If
possible, try to make sure that when all three
of you are together, you all take it in turns
when you have to do things in pairs. If nothing
changes after that, then maybe they are not
worth being friends with, especially if they
make you feel bad and ignore your feelings.

If you feel things aren't working, you should

try to find ways of widening your circle of friends, so that when you do go out, the problem of the 'threesome' doesn't arise. If there were four of you, for example, you could automatically divide up into pairs.

Best wishes *Aunty*

☆ ☆ ☆ ☆ ☆

Dear Aunty

My best friend and I were friends for the whole time we were at primary school. But now we are at secondary school, she has started being nasty to me, and telling me what to do all the time. She has started hanging out with other girls and they all seem to laugh at me. She whispers things to these new friends and I am sure they are talking about me. She has one new special friend she sits next to in class. What shall I do?

Emily, aged 11

Dear Emily

Unfortunately when you start a new school, it often happens that old friends may change for no real reason. Maybe your friend just wants to make new friends and keep you at a distance for a while. Well, rather than worrying about this, you can make new friends too. Channel all your efforts into meeting girls who you feel have something in common with you – girls who share the same interests, girls who might live near you that you can meet outside school.

Try not to worry about your old best friend. You can keep her at a distance too, for a while. When she sees how popular you are with your new friends, she may come round in the end, and even if she doesn't, your other friends will be there for you instead.

Best wishes   *Aunty*

☆ ☆ ☆ ☆ ☆

Dear Aunty

My family have just moved house, and I have started a new secondary school. I am really shy and am finding it quite difficult to make new friends. What can I do?

Stella, aged 11

Dear Stella

This is a difficult situation for anyone finding herself in a new setting. It can be really difficult to make the first approach to a group of strangers. You need a lot of courage. You could take a deep breath, and just go up to a group of girls, introduce yourself and see what happens.

One good way of making friends is to join one of the after-school clubs, such as the drama group. Acting is a good way of overcoming your shyness and you are bound to make new friends in the process.

Best wishes *Aunty*

Dear Aunty

I have had a terrible row with my best friend at school, and we haven't spoken to each other for over a week. I was teasing her about some boy I think she fancies, and she got really annoyed with me. I got annoyed back and we screamed at each other. I was really surprised about how angry we both were.

What can I do?

Sonia, aged 12

Dear Sonia

Rows with your best friend are not unusual. At your age, your emotions can be all over the place, you might get angry and lose your temper, and next thing you know you're not speaking to your best friend. Maybe you need to think that what you said might have upset her. You have to swallow your pride and make the first move. Why not ring her at home in the evening and suggest going shopping or visiting the cinema? Alternatively, you could send her a note asking if you can be friends again. I am sure she is just as miserable as you are.

Best wishes   *Aunty*

Families

Dear Aunty

My parents are always rowing. They are always shouting and screaming at each other. Sometimes they argue about really silly things. Is it my fault? How can I stop them?

Anita, aged 13

Dear Anita

Unfortunately most of the time you may not be able to do anything about your parents' rows. It might be that they are having problems with their relationship and things are not right between them at the moment. Remember, please, this has nothing to do with you – IT IS NOT YOUR FAULT. There is no guarantee that couples – in this case, your parents – will have a magic formula for being happy all the time. You can't stop your parents from rowing, and you must try not to take sides. The only thing you can do is tell them that you are worried about them and that their arguments upset you a lot. See what they have to say. If your parents rows do not get any better, they might try a Relate counsellor who will try and make things better between them. The telephone number is at the back of the book.

Best wishes *Aunty*

☆ ☆ ☆ ☆ ☆

Dear Aunty

My parents are getting a divorce. They have talked about what will happen after the divorce. I will be living with my mum and my brother, and we are staying in our house, and my dad is moving to a new job in a new town. I am scared that I won't see my dad any more.

Kylie, aged 12

Dear Kylie

Divorce can be very stressful, especially for the children involved. It can be a very distressing experience, I'm afraid. Children are always stuck in the middle through no fault of their own. Divorce can affect many people, and it is most likely that some of your school friends are in the same position as yourself. Do try to talk to them about it if you can.

Hopefully, your parents will come to an amicable arrangement about your dad's parental contact. Even if they cannot agree about this between themselves, your feelings and your opinion will be taken into account. Sometimes parental contact is decided by a court, and the judge should ensure you and your father's views are taken into account. If he is moving a long way away, the most likely thing will be that you will see him at pre-arranged times, for instance during holidays, and maybe for some weekends. And don't forget you can telephone him, write to him, or e-mail him any time you wish. Make sure he has an e-mail address when he moves to his new home. The likelihood is that he may be on e-mail at his new job, but it would be better to contact him at home, and you can keep him up to date with your life, and even confide in him about any worries you may have.

Best wishes *Aunty*

☆ ☆ ☆ ☆ ☆

Dear Aunty

My parents are divorced. Every weekend I go and stay with my dad but I hate my step-mother. I can't bear her, and it's not just because I think she's not as nice or as pretty as my mum is. She's always sucking up to my dad, but she's just pretending. Underneath it all she makes him do exactly what she wants. And he's always buying her presents. I hate her so much, I don't want to spend my weekends with her.

Briony, aged 10

Dear Briony

Lots of people will sympathise with you. It is difficult to form a good relationship with your step-parents. Unfortunately stepmothers traditionally do get rather a bad press. However, there are lots of girls in a similar boat as you, and basically, you just have to take a deep breath and try to get on with her.

Your feelings of jealousy towards your stepmother are understandable, but what about your dad? She must have some redeeming qualities or your dad wouldn't have married her, and he does love her, obviously. Notice I use the word 'love'. If you love your dad, and want to keep seeing him, then for his sake, try at least to make an effort. In this life I am afraid nothing is clear-cut, and you obviously feel very protective towards your mother. Your feelings for your step-mother may never be warm, but you will have to learn how to act in a civilised manner towards her. Show you are mature and try to get on with her. You may even end up liking her, so try to give it a go at least.

If you find things don't improve, then have a

word with your dad. See if there are any other solutions, but don't give him an ultimatum, you'll probably lose out.

Best wishes *Aunty*

☆ ☆ ☆ ☆ ☆

Dear Aunty

I never got on with my dad, and when he started hitting my mum, that was the end as far as I was concerned. Now he and mum are divorced. I don't really want to see him any more, but when my parents got divorced, the court judge said my dad had to have contact. When he comes to see me, once a month, I don't really know what to say to him. I can't forgive him for hitting my mum.

Nadia, aged 12

Dear Nadia

This is very difficult for you. Maybe you could try to approach your dad and discuss the way you feel with him. If you have the courage, try to ask him why he used to hit your mum. Some men hit women and truly regret it later. It might help if you could talk about it with him. You many never forgive him for hitting your mum but there may be good things about him you are too angry to see at the moment.

   If you still find you're not getting on better with him, it might be possible to go back to court and get the contact reduced. When you are older it will be up to you whether you want to continue to see him or not. You need to think long and hard about this. Do you really want a life where you will never see him again? It might help if you had some legal advice on this troublesome matter.

Best wishes   *Aunty*

Dear Aunty

My brother is really mean to me. He's nearly 17 and I am 13, and he never lets me go out with him. He's always telling me off and taking the mickey out of my hair and my clothes. When his friends come round to the house, he always tells me to get out of the way. Why isn't he nicer to me?

Clementine, aged 13

Dear Clementine

Your brother is four years older than you are, so for him this is quite a big age gap. He is trying to act grown up so he doesn't want to be seen with younger girls. It's all to do with male adolescence. Boys, as well as girls, have lots of problems when they are growing up. They get spots, their voices change, they start growing facial hair, their bodies seem to grow out of all proportion. Boys try desperately hard to be masculine, to prove that they are hard and uncaring, and younger sisters can bear the brunt of it. Your brother may be insensitive to you because he's completely wrapped up in himself at the moment. Try some confusing tactics. Be as nice to him as possible. Compliment him on his appearance or clothes; ask him if he needs anything; run errands for him. And when his friends come round, be polite to them, but keep out of their way, and don't try 'tagging' on. Your brother will be so astounded, he will be speechless!

Best wishes *Aunty*

☆ ☆ ☆ ☆ ☆

Dear Aunty

I hate my younger sister. I am 11 and she is 9. She's really thin and she's much prettier than I am. She does really well at school, while I always seem to be struggling to keep up with the others in the class. It's not fair, and every time I try to talk to my mum about it, she tells me not to worry. Most of the time I shout at my sister, and even my mum, and I don't know what to do about it. Help!

Marguerite, aged 11

Dear Marguerite

Your mum is right, try not to worry about this. It's only you who thinks your sister is prettier and cleverer than you are. And please don't even think about her being thinner. She's younger than you are, so she's bound to be thinner. A girl's weight can go up and down like a Yo-Yo. It is very difficult to judge whether you will end up thin or fat, as you grow older. And really, you shouldn't worry too much.

If you haven't already, you will be changing schools soon. Try to look forward to a new challenge and a new life. Some girls really flourish in their teens. You may well catch up with your schoolmates, and even if you don't, it doesn't really matter. Your mum loves you just as much as your sister. She loves you for what you are. And think of your sister. Don't shout at her. You may even miss her when you go to your new school. Please try to remember that sisters do need each other, even though you don't think so at the moment. Try to think what you would do if somebody tried to hurt your sister in any way. As the older sister, I am sure you would do all you could to protect her.

Best wishes   *Aunty*

Growing Up

Dear Aunty

It is really easy for me to walk home from school as I only live less than a mile away. Some of my friends walk home, but my mum always insists on picking me up in the car. How can I persuade her to let me walk home from school?

Halima, aged 12

Dear Halima

Maybe the first step would be for you to ask your mum to walk to the school to pick you up. You could then both walk home, which would give you both some exercise, and save on adding to the traffic at the same time! Only when your mum is convinced that you are safe will she let you walk home on your own. If you have a school friend who lives nearby, you could both walk to and from school together, which would be even better. That would most probably put your mum's mind at rest. Talk to your mother and see what she thinks of ideas like these. I'm sure you will find a compromise, but don't push her too hard to agree with you. Sometimes being patient is the best way.

Best wishes *Aunty*

☆ ☆ ☆ ☆ ☆

Dear Aunty

All my friends are allowed to watch television during the week until 9.30 p.m. I am 11, and the latest I am ever allowed up is 8.30 p.m. There are lots of TV programmes I would love to see, as all my friends talk about them at school. What time should I go to bed?

Nathalie, aged 11

Dear Nathalie

Well, you do need to have a lot of sleep at your age, and when you have school in the morning it is a very good idea to get to bed early. Some TV programmes shown after 8 p.m. and before 9 p.m. are not suitable for children in any case. Your parents may decide what you can and cannot watch. Maybe you could negotiate with your parents to watch television until 9 p.m. on certain evenings, say Friday and Saturday. And you could always video the programmes you want to see and watch them at weekends. Some programmes are even repeated, quite often at the weekends. Do please make sure that you do all your homework first, before you start watching television!

Best wishes   *Aunty*

☆ ☆ ☆ ☆ ☆

Dear Aunty

What time should I be allowed to stay out to on my own? I am nearly 13, and my dad always insists on coming with me to see a band or concert and I find it very embarrassing.

Emma, aged 12

Dear Emma

The time you are allowed to stay out is really up to your parents and nobody else. It also really depends on your age and where you live. On no account should you go out on your own. Always make sure that you are with a friend, and that your parents know who you're with and where you are going. It's difficult to say how long you should stay out, especially in winter, when it gets dark at 5 p.m.! Obviously the younger you are, the earlier you should come in. But as I said before, it's really up to your parents.

   Going to see a band or a concert can be quite scary. They are often held in large spaces, and can be intimidating and very noisy. They also usually end very late in the evening. I would say it is a good idea for a parent or adult to accompany you to such places. If this is too embarrassing for you, maybe an older sister or the older sister of a friend, or another relative could come with you.

Best wishes   *Aunty*

☆ ☆ ☆ ☆ ☆

Dear Aunty

One of my dad's friends is always trying to touch me. He always cuddles me and hugs me when he sees me and one day when he came to a party at my parents' house, he kissed me on the lips and told me it was our little secret. I didn't know what to do.

Susie, aged 12

Dear Susie

You must tell your parents about their friend. They should have a word with him and discourage him from visiting your house any longer. Hopefully, you will never have to see him. If this ever happens to you again, and an adult tries to kiss you, you must say 'no' in a very loud voice. If they persist, you should carry on making a lot of noise, and run off for help.

Unfortunately there are some adults who like children in a sexual way. They can be very disturbed and dangerous people, and must be avoided.

If you ever see this man again, try to avoid him at all costs. If he gets you alone, tell him to get lost, and if he touches you, tell him you will tell your parents, or his wife, if he has one. Try not to be frightened by him, just keep as far away from him as possible. If you and your parents need advice about how to deal with this very worrying problem, you can contact ChildLine on 0800 1111.

Best wishes *Aunty*

Dear Aunty

My parents won't let me out during the week, which is really annoying, as there is always a disco on every Tuesday in the local community centre. Why can't I go to it?

Ngosi, aged 13

Dear Ngosi

It can be difficult for parents to let their children out during the week. You have school the next day, so they will be worried about you going out in the evening before a school day. You will have homework to do, and will have to get up early for school the next day.

Maybe you could reach a compromise and ask your parents if it would be OK to go to the disco during the school holidays.

Best wishes   *Aunty*

Dear Aunty

We live in the middle of the country so it is very difficult for me to go out into town in the evenings, even at the weekends. My parents will not allow me to go out on my own into town, and sometimes it is really difficult for them to give me a lift. So some weekends I don't go out at all, and I am stuck at home. How can I get out more?

Claudia, aged 13

Dear Claudia

Sometimes living in the country can be difficult for girls who are keen to go out at weekends. Your parents are obviously worried about your safety, and getting a bus (if there is one running) on one's own can be dangerous. The only thing I can suggest is that you arrange for one of your friend's parents to come and pick you up and take you back, if your parents can't manage to do it themselves. Alternatively, you could arrange to stay the night with a friend who lives in the town, but your parents would have to be very sure that they know the girl, her parents, and where she lives, before they allow you to do this. Always make sure that your parents and your friend's parents discuss this possibility in advance. Your parents should keep a note of your friend's telephone number and your friend's parents should have a note of yours. You should ring your parents when you get to your friend's house, and ring them again the following morning, either to confirm what time your friend's parents are taking you back home, or alternatively, what time your parents are coming to pick you up.

Best wishes   *Aunty*

Body Changes

Dear Aunty

I am 11 and my mum says I will be going through puberty soon. What does it mean exactly?

Gemma, aged 11

Dear Gemma

Puberty is when a girl's body changes into a woman's body. Certain things happen. Your breasts get bigger, your hips and thighs get wider and rounder, you start to sweat more, and your body smell might change, so you may need to use a deodorant. You grow hair around the genitals and armpits and all over your body generally. You will grow in spurts, and get taller and put on weight. Your skin will also change and unfortunately you may suffer from spots and acne. The most noticeable sign is when your ovaries begin releasing eggs and menstruation (periods) starts.

Best wishes *Aunty*

☆ ☆ ☆ ☆ ☆

Dear Aunty

Sometimes I shout and scream at my mum for no reason. She tells me not to worry, it's all to do with my hormones. What does she mean exactly?

Holly, aged 12

Dear Holly

During puberty, the body is preparing itself for the time when a woman may have a baby. In order for sexual reproduction to take place, men and women have to produce sexual hormones. In girls, the female hormone, oestrogen, is produced in the ovaries, and in boys, the male hormone, testosterone, is produced in the testicles. Hormones are chemicals made in the blood. They act like internal chemical messengers, and sometimes they can send out confusing signals to the brain, which make us feel stressed and emotional.

During puberty when the production of the sex hormones begins, your emotions and moods can be very much affected. There are many expressions about hormones. Very often people say adolescents act in a certain way because their hormones are rushing about all over the place. Both boys and girls can appear moody and uncommunicative. One minute you can be feeling really happy, the next minute you can be deeply depressed. This can lead to rows and arguments, without you really understanding what is happening to you. But don't worry too much – this is all part of the process of growing up. Your hormones do affect the way you behave during adolescence, but this should settle down eventually.

Best wishes   *Aunty*

Dear Aunty

I am worried about my breasts. My nipples seem to itch all the time and I am sure one breast is bigger than the other is.

Samantha, aged 13

Dear Samantha

Breasts and nipples do tingle or itch while they're growing, but this will stop when they reach their full size. Growth in each breast can be uneven, so that one breast looks bigger than the other does. Don't worry, this will usually even out. But many women have slightly different sized breasts and this is very normal.

Best wishes   *Aunty*

Dear Aunty

None of the girls in my class wear a bra yet,
but I am getting quite big and my mum says we
should go shopping for a bra. I am really
embarrassed about this. And how do I know
what bra size I need?

Victoria, aged 11

Dear Victoria

I know you must feel self-conscious about
your breasts, especially if you are the first girl
in your class to get a bra. But look upon it as
a privilege to be the first. You will be able to
tell your friends all about it. After all, you will
know something they don't know about.

It is very important to wear a bra straight
away as it will help your breasts to stay firm
and keep a nice shape for later in life. It is
very important to get a good fitting bra. Some
underwear shops or department stores offer
a free measuring service so you can get the
bra that's right for you.

Alternatively, you can measure yourself. To find out what bra size you are, use a tape measure with inches, around your chest just underneath your breasts. This will be the actual size in inches of the bra you need. If this is an even number of inches, add 4 inches to that number. If it is an odd number, add 5 inches. Then measure the fullest part of your breasts. If the two numbers are the same, you need an A-cup. If there's a 1-inch difference you need a B-cup. If there's a 2-inch difference, you need a C-cup, and if there's a 3-inch difference, you need a D-cup, and so on. Make sure you check your measurements every few months, so that you know your bra is the right size for you.

Best wishes   *Aunty*

☆ ☆ ☆ ☆ ☆

Dear Aunty

All my friends are getting breasts and I'm not. The boys at school tease me and call me flat chested. I'm really worried and I am seriously thinking about stuffing paper hankies down my jumper to stop the boys getting at me. Help!

Kate, aged 13

Dear Kate

Please try not to be too unhappy about this. Girls develop breasts at different times, and there are many girls like you who have to wait a while longer. Talk to your mum about it. Maybe she had to wait a while for her breasts to grow as well. But don't worry, it's quite normal. And these days, you can buy very fashionable padded bras. I'm sure your mum will help you buy one.

Try to ignore the boys, they are being very immature. I bet they have hidden fears about their bits too!

Best wishes   *Aunty*

Dear Aunty

I hate my appearance. I'm 13 and putting on lots of weight, especially around my thighs. Should I go on a diet?

Jane, aged 13

Dear Jane

You do a lot of growing during your teens so your body fat and muscle will increase. This can be known as 'puppy fat'. As you change from a girl to a woman, you'll usually get taller, your hips will get broader and your thighs and buttocks will get fatter. If you are tall or have a large frame you will weigh more than if you are short or have a small frame. Periods also affect your weight. But please, please don't go on a diet. You are too young. It's OK to eat all the foods that you enjoy, just as long as you eat plenty of fruit and vegetables as well. If you need to eat between meals, try a carrot or celery, an apple, some nuts, Ryvita or a cereal bar.

Exercise is also a good way of trying to control your weight. So get that bike out — cycling is especially good for thighs.

Best wishes *Aunty*

☆ ☆ ☆ ☆ ☆

Dear Aunty

I have started to get pubic hair and hair under my arms, and I can see hairs growing on my legs. I hate it, what can I do?

Fran, aged 12

Dear Fran

All women have body hair. During adolescence pubic hair appears around the genitals first, then hair grows in the armpits, on the legs and sometimes on other parts of the body. Some women choose to shave, wax or use creams to remove hair on their legs or under their arms and others don't. It's a matter of personal choice, and it can also depend on which culture you come from. Some Muslim women remove all their bodily hair, while some European women never touch it. Some people find underarm hair and even hairy legs sexy, so the choice is yours.

I have one handy hint for you. If the hair on your legs remains quite fine, don't touch it. If you start to shave, the hairs will get coarser and thicker, and once you start shaving your legs, you won't be able to stop. If you do want to remove any hair, it might be better to wax than to shave, even though it can be more painful.

Best wishes   *Aunty*

Periods

Dear Aunty

Why do I have to have periods? I hate them!

Chantalle, aged 13

Dear Chantalle

Periods are a normal, healthy part of being a woman and pretty soon, you should hopefully be more relaxed about them. At puberty, a girl releases an egg every month. The hormone, oestrogen, causes this. On average a woman will release 400 to 500 eggs from her ovaries during her lifetime. This is called ovulation. You have to ovulate to get pregnant. Most of these eggs, however, do not get fertilised and are therefore shed from the body. Every month the womb prepares itself for a fertilised egg and produces a thicker spongy lining. If the egg is not fertilised, your hormones cause the lining to disintegrate and the lining passes through the cervix and vagina as bleeding – this is called 'menstruation' or 'having a period'.

When you are older and you want to get pregnant, you will know that ovulating and menstruating every month means that your body is ready for pregnancy. Having periods can be annoying but if you didn't have them, it would mean that something might be wrong.

Best wishes *Aunty*

☆ ☆ ☆ ☆ ☆

Dear Aunty

How long does a period usually last? I'm sure there is something wrong with me because mine only last three days.

Kin Yee, aged 14

Dear Kin Yee

A period normally lasts about five days. On the first two days, the blood flow is usually heavier than for the rest of the period. However, some-times they can go on for a week or 10 days, and for some people like you, periods can only last about three days, so please don't worry.

Best wishes *Aunty*

☆ ☆ ☆ . ☆ ☆

Dear Aunty

I started my period for the first time the other day. I was really shocked to see the blood. How will I know when my next period will start?

Trudie, aged 12

Dear Trudie

Starting your periods for the first time can be a shock but it is something that you will get used to. It's what makes women special.

When you first start having periods, it might be difficult for you to work out when your next period will be as they might take some time to settle into a regular pattern. Your periods may not be regular to start with. At the beginning, some girls sometimes have to wait quite a while for their next period.

Your period is connected to your menstrual cycle. The menstrual cycle is calculated from the first day of a period until the day before the next period starts. The length of the menstrual cycle varies – it can be as short as 21 days or as long as 40 days, but is usually around 28 days. When you first have a period, the time between one period and the next may vary, so it can be difficult to know when you will have your next period. When your menstrual cycle becomes more regular you can use a diary to work out when your next period is due. However, be prepared – carry sanitary towels, small and discreet, around the time your period is due.

Best wishes *Aunty*

Dear Aunty

I feel really awful just before I start a period?
Is this normal?

Bea, aged 13

Dear Bea

Hormones, especially the hormone oestrogen,
produced in the ovaries, control the menstrual
cycle and they can affect your moods as well,
depending on what stage you have reached in
your cycle. It is quite normal to feel moody,
tearful or angry in the week before your
period is due. There may be physical changes
as well. Breasts may become a bit larger and you
may get spots on your face just before a period.
You should eat lots of fresh fruit and vegetables,
and don't eat too much sugar or salt. It is a
good idea to take regular exercise, which can
help a lot, both mentally and physically.

Best wishes   *Aunty*

Dear Aunty

I hate wearing sanitary pads. I find it really difficult changing pads, especially when I'm at school. Sometimes I just stuff loads of loo paper over my old pad. I find the whole thing really difficult. Help!

Yasmin, aged 13

Dear Yasmin

I know periods can be a pain, but you really should try to change your pads every few hours. If you don't, they start to smell. Loo paper is not secure enough, and the blood might seep on to your clothes. If you are worried that somebody will see you throwing away your pad, there are many pads that are thin and discreet and come with wrappers, which make disposal easy. Roll the pad up (sticky side up) and put it inside the wrapper. All you have to do is put it in the bin in the loo, or the nearest bin you can find. Also remember that all women have been through what you're going through. It's completely normal to be worried but relax, and once you get into the routine, it won't seem so difficult after all.

Best wishes *Aunty*

☆ ☆ ☆ ☆ ☆

Dear Aunty

Should I use sanitary pads or tampons when I start my first period?

Vanessa, aged 11

Dear Vanessa

It's most probably a good idea to start off with sanitary pads. They are easier to use. You just follow the instructions on the packet, and companies like Always even have leaflets, which they will send out to you. You can experiment with a few different makes and decide which ones suit you best. The best ones these days have a self-adhesive strip, which easily sticks to your panties and stays in position. Some even have wings which stay in position even better. The thickness of the towel you need depends on how heavy your period is. For the first day or two it is better to use a thicker towel, then by the end of your period a panty-liner will most probably be sufficient. When you become accustomed to your period, there is no reason why you shouldn't be able to use tampons as well.

Best wishes *Aunty*

☆ ☆ ☆ ☆ ☆

Dear Aunty

I am 12 and going on holiday to France. I am really worried about having my period when I get there, and I really want to go swimming as we are going to be at the seaside. What can I do?

Tessa, aged 12

Dear Tessa

To enable you to go swimming it would be a good idea to buy a packet of tampons, before you leave for France, and practise with them. Please try to discuss this with your mum or an adult you know well. Your mum or friend can tell you which sort to get. There are two kinds: ones with an applicator tube, and ones without. At your age, it's most probably better to start with applicator tampons. You can buy mini, regular, super or super plus tampons. Again discuss this with your mum, but to begin with, you could try mini or regular. If you find these get soaked very quickly, then use super for the first two or three days of your period.

To find out how they work, immerse a tampon in lukewarm water and see how it expands. The same thing will happen inside your vagina, and the tampon will soak up the blood. Practise putting one in. You need to be as relaxed as possible. If it is your first time putting one in, you will be tense, so try lying down, or standing with one leg on a chair. Be careful to follow the instructions on the packet very carefully. *And* please be sure to change your tampons regularly, at least every four to six hours.

Best wishes   *Aunty*

Appearance

Dear Aunty

Just when I am about to get ready to go to a party, I always seem to discover a spot right in the middle of my forehead or on my nose. How can I stop this happening?

Uma, aged 14

Dear Uma

Girls are always very aware of their own spots and blemishes. It's quite likely that other people can't even notice your spots. However, if you are really worried about your spots, there are a couple of things that you can do. If you have a spot on your forehead, you can always cover it with your hair, especially if your hair is cut with a fringe, but you must ensure that both your skin and hair are very clean. Alternatively, if you have a spot on your nose, you can wear a touch of make-up over it. There are several products on the market, like cover-up sticks, for example, but make sure you buy a reputable make. And again, please ensure your skin is really clean before applying make-up.

Best wishes *Aunty*

☆ ☆ ☆ ☆ ☆

Dear Aunty

I've got lots of blackheads on my face. I've tried lots of different products. Some of them are really expensive and most seem to make my skin look worse. What can I do?

Babs, aged 13

Dear Babs

Blackheads are caused by blocked-up pores on the skin, especially the face. There are a

million remedies on the market, but you can't try them all. One good way of getting rid of black heads is to put your face over a bowl of boiling water. The steam from the water will help loosen the pores. Make sure you wash with cold water afterwards, and then use an alcohol-free skin toner.

As you get older and finish puberty, you will find you will get much fewer blackheads. Good luck!

Best wishes   *Aunty*

☆ ☆ ☆ ☆ ☆

Dear Aunty

I have lots of spots, especially on my back. I feel really embarrassed by them, especially when I wear a swimsuit and I never dare wear a low-backed top. What can I do?

Zandra, aged 14

Dear Zandra

Everyone has spots at one time or other, especially on their backs. Just make sure you wash your back regularly with pure vegetable soap and water. In summer, it's quite a good idea to get some mild sunshine on your back. So do put on your swimsuit and get out to that garden or park. Try and get 20 or 30 minutes of sun a day. But whatever skin colour you are, please be careful not to stay out too long, and make sure you wear some sun-cream protection. After a while you should be able to stay in the sun longer, your spots should improve and you will be able to wear low-backed tops. But as I said before, please make sure that you don't overdo that sunbathing.

Best wishes   *Aunty*

☆ ☆ ☆ ☆ ☆

Dear Aunty

I am really tall for my age, and I am much taller than my boyfriend is. We are both 13, and sometimes I can hear people at school laughing behind our backs, and they call us 'Little and Large'.

Tammy, aged 13

Dear Tammy

Please don't worry about this. Your boyfriend obviously doesn't mind. All boys and girls grow at different rates. Some people stop growing at 12; some don't stop growing until they are 20 or more. Some of your friends and even your boyfriend might catch you up one day. But does it really matter? You should be pleased you are tall. Men find tall women very attractive. What about Tom Cruise and Nicole Kidman?

Best wishes   *Aunty*

Dear Aunty

I am 14 and really tall for my age – 6 foot,
1 inch. Lots of people tell me I could become a
model, but I am really shy and being tall makes
me feel really unconfident. I am much taller
than all the girls and most of the boys in my
year, and I find it difficult to find clothes that
fit me, especially jeans and trousers. Where can
I go?

Naomi, aged 14

Dear Naomi

It's wonderful to be tall, and I am sure you are
a very attractive girl.
   If you are having problems with clothes,
there are shops that specialise in clothing for
tall people. For instance there is a chain of
shops called Long Tall Sally. Alternatively you
could look at buying boys' clothes which are
usually just as fashionable and cool as girls'
clothes, especially jeans and trousers.
Otherwise you could look up some sites on

the Internet, which specialise in things for tall people.

Best wishes *Aunty*

☆ ☆ ☆ ☆ ☆

Dear Aunty

I can't stop biting my nails. They look really ugly and the more I worry about them, the more I bite them. Sometimes they start bleeding, and they really hurt.

Nadine, aged 11

Dear Nadine

Lots of girls bite their nails during adolescence. And it is very difficult to stop. Sometimes it's just a question of will-power. You have to sit up one morning in bed and say to yourself very firmly, 'Today I will *stop* biting my nails.' Ask your family and school-mates to help you as well. Every time they see you biting your nails, they should say, 'Stop', as loud as they can.

There are some nail-biting prevention products that you can buy in good chemists. They are usually similar to nail varnish. You paint the liquid on to your nails. The smell and taste is so disgusting it's supposed to put you off biting them. There are nail-strengthening preparations as well, which are also like nail varnish. Sometimes people who bite their nails are tempted to bite off a nail when it's torn or broken. These nail-strengthening products help you to look after your nails, and help them grow at the same time.

Best wishes *Aunty*

☆ ☆ ☆ ☆ ☆

Dear Aunty

My hair is really greasy. It's long and lank, and I hate it. What can I do with it?

Georgia, aged 12

Dear Georgia

Greasy hair is a common problem. The best thing to do is to wash it at least every two days. There are lots of shampoos on the market, but I would say ones for normal or greasy hair are the best. You might not feel like washing your hair this often, but because your hair has lots of natural oil it will look lovely and healthy when you wash it regularly. And because your hair is naturally oily, you don't need to use a conditioner, so that will save time!

If your hair is long, it's a good idea to get it cut on a regular basis. This will keep your hair free from split ends and make it look thicker as well.

Best wishes   *Aunty*

Dear Aunty

I always brush my teeth regularly but they look very yellow. How can I make them look whiter?

Yolande, aged 13

Dear Yolande

It is quite common to have yellow teeth, and in fact, some people's teeth are naturally more yellow than others. However to keep your teeth in tiptop condition, you should make sure you brush your teeth for three minutes morning and night. You should also use dental floss at least three times a week and make sure you visit the dentist every six months. Your dentist might be able to offer a solution about yellow teeth, and the dental hygienist will clean your teeth and make them look as good as possible. Remember that up to the age of 16 dental care is free on the NHS, so make the most of it!

There are also some toothpastes available to whiten teeth but I'm not sure that they are really effective. Tea and coffee also stain, so try not to drink more than two cups of either a day, and whatever you do, don't smoke, this is the worst cause ever of yellow teeth!

Best wishes   *Aunty*

Health Issues

Dear Aunty

My best friend smokes and she is always offering me cigarettes. My parents are always telling me not to smoke, as it's bad for my health, but I am curious. Why shouldn't I smoke?

Wendy, aged 14

Dear Wendy

There is a lot of pressure on young people to smoke. Some girls think it is cool and grown up, but a lot of people will say that they wish they had never started. Smoking is really bad for your health and can lead to heart disease, strokes and cancer when you are older. In the long term it can lead to pinched lips and greyish skin.

Rather than wondering what it's like to

smoke yourself, you should concentrate on trying to persuade your friend to give up smoking. You should make sure that she never smokes in your house, or when she is with you in a public place, and best of all, remind her about the smell. Some people's hair and clothes are always smelly, and this is because they smoke. And what about bad breath? Smoking is the main cause of smelly breath. And you and your friend should think about this fact – boys don't like kissing girls with bad breath, that's for sure.

When you are young, it's not that difficult to give up smoking but as you get older, it becomes more and more difficult. So please don't try smoking yourself and try to make your friend give up too.

Best wishes   *Aunty*

☆ ☆ ☆ ☆ ☆

Dear Aunty

I keep on wetting myself, especially if I sneeze, laugh or cough. I just can't help it. I am 14 and it's been going on for a year. I am really worried about it, but I'm too embarrassed to say anything to my mum. I try holding it in, but it doesn't work. What can I do?

Daisy, aged 14

Dear Daisy

I know you must be very worried, but it is quite a common problem for girls of your age. In fact one in ten girls can be affected. Weak muscles in your abdomen usually cause it. These muscles give way when you sneeze, laugh, cough, run or lift things. But if you try some simple pelvic floor exercises, your muscles will be strengthened, and this should do the trick.

Using your muscles down below, try to pull up your front and back passages tightly (as if trying to stop the bowels from opening), hold tight for a count of four and relax. Repeat this for 15 minutes each morning before you go to school or before you go to bed at night. You should also go and see the nurse at your local GP's surgery or health centre. She can check that everything is OK, and give you a leaflet about pelvic floor exercises. In the meantime wear panty liners in case of accidents, and carry on with the exercises until you notice a difference.

Best wishes *Aunty*

☆ ☆ ☆ ☆ ☆

Dear Aunty

How can I eat a healthy diet? When I am at school it's really tempting to eat lots of sweets and crisps.

Helen, aged 13

Dear Helen

Eating a healthy diet is quite simple. You need to cut out animal fat, sugar and salt. Eat as much fresh fruit and as many fresh vegetables as you can. Rather than having a snack that involves sweets, biscuits, cake or crisps, eat an apple, banana or orange. You should really eat fruit or vegetables five times a day. So fruit for breakfast and morning breaktime, vegetables at lunch and dinner and fruit for your afternoon snack. Drink lots of water to go with them. Potatoes, brown bread and pasta are also good for you, and as you are still growing, you need calcium for healthy bones. So drink between half a pint to one pint of milk a day. Cheese and yoghurt are also high in calcium. Finally, lean meat and fish are good for you, but you don't have to eat them every day, and try not to eat things like sausages and bacon, which are very fatty.

There have been some studies about schools that have stopped selling junk food like fizzy drinks and crisps. Remarkably, these schools' exam grades have greatly increased, so don't forget this when you are next tempted.

Best wishes *Aunty*

☆ ☆ ☆ ☆ ☆

Dear Aunty

I have terrible toothache all the time, but I am really scared of going to the dentist.

Dee, aged 13

Dear Dee

You must try and overcome your fear of going to the dentist. It is very important that your teeth are checked regularly. And it sounds like you do need help. Have a word with your parents, or maybe your GP can recommend a good dentist who will be sympathetic. You can explain your anxieties and I am sure the dentist will do everything to make you feel comfortable and relaxed.

If you go to the dentist regularly, tiny problems can be sorted out before they become big problems. If you are getting toothache, you may have a hole in your tooth, so please avoid anything too hot, too cold or too sweet. The dentist might decide that you need a filling. The dentist will fill the hole with a type of plastic that should stop it getting any worse. And, don't worry, you will hardly feel a thing. These days, going to the dentist isn't so bad after all.

Best wishes *Aunty*

Dear Aunty

Everybody is always going on about how to keep fit and healthy, but I don't know what it really means to be fit and healthy.

Fern, aged 14

Dear Fern

Well, you can keep fit and healthy in a variety of ways. It doesn't necessarily mean playing a sport. You can keep fit by walking to school, dancing, or even helping with the housework. But if you do fancy the idea of sport or exercise, you could try swimming, aerobics, football and best of all, cycling. This will help you to stop putting on weight, make you think clearer and most importantly, keep you healthy. But remember a good diet is an essential part of keeping fit, and you should get a good night's sleep as well. Girls of your age may need about nine hours of sleep a night, so remember that before you decide to stay up late to watch television.

Best wishes   *Aunty*

☆ ☆ ☆ ☆ ☆

Dear Aunty

I am sure I am overweight. I want to go on a diet. Which one should I choose?

Faith, aged 14

Dear Faith

You are most probably not medically over-weight so please don't go on a diet, just follow a healthy diet, as I've mentioned previously in this section. A lot of girls put on weight during puberty. They become rounder, and their bodies look more adult-like. When you get older, it's just as likely that you will end up thin because your weight does fluctuate. And please remember dieting can be dangerous.

Rather than going on a diet, try and do some more exercise. Ask your parents or PE teacher if there are any keep fit classes that you can join.

Best wishes   *Aunty*

Emotions

Dear Aunty

I am 14 and I seem to find life really stressful.
I worry about how I look, the world, school, my
parents, my friends and what they think of me,
and well, just about everything. Things just seem
to get on top of me all the time.

What can I do?

Stacey, aged 14

Dear Stacey

Modern life is quite stressful, whether you're at
school, university or work. There are always
worries and problems to cope with, and things
never run smoothly. Most young people worry
– especially girls. So you shouldn't worry about
worrying! It is very normal and most of us will
worry about personal problems for the rest of

our lives. Things like money, families and work will always be a concern.

However, you are very young, and you shouldn't be feeling that all the troubles of the world are on your shoulders. Have you thought about what you could do in your spare time? Maybe taking up a very active sport might help, or getting involved with the local community, as a volunteer, might take your mind off things.

If things don't improve, you could seek advice from your GP.

Best wishes   *Aunty*

☆ ☆ ☆ ☆ ☆

Dear Aunty

Sometimes I hate myself and feel that other people don't like me. I seem to feel very depressed all the time, and can't stop crying. What is the matter with me?

Pattie, aged 13

Dear Pattie

Sometimes girls do have quite low self-esteem, especially during puberty. Self-esteem is important, and even if a girl is good-looking and clever, she may not feel she is. She may think she is ugly and stupid and no good at anything. Unfortunately, feeling like this is all part of the process of growing up. You normally grow out of it.

   Sometimes, however, depression can be a clinical illness. If you think you need help, you should have a word with your parents about this, or maybe a teacher you like at school. You could also have a chat to your GP. You might think about seeing a counsellor. You would need to feel comfortable about seeing such a person, and you will need to stick with it for a few months. Look for details on the British Association for Counselling at the back of the book. Whatever you are depressed about, it can usually be sorted out, no matter how bad you think it is. If you are diagnosed as having 'clinical' depression then this may require medication of some kind.

Best wishes   *Aunty*

Dear Aunty

Every so often I get really emotional, and shout and scream at everybody. It seems to happen before I start my period. Why am I like this?

Joanna, aged 14

Dear Joanna

Lots of women get stressed out before a period. There is even a name for it. It is called premenstrual syndrome or PMS. Sometimes it can be quite a problem, but at your age it should be manageable. PMS usually starts after you've been having periods for quite a while, when your cycle has settled down into a regular pattern. You will learn to recognise what part of your cycle you've reached, so you should come to expect the times of the month you might find stressful. Try and relax as much as you can, even deep breathing might help.

You could try yoga or some gentle exercise. If you find it's getting no better, please contact your doctor. There are also some herbal remedies on the market, such as evening primrose oil, and vitamins such as B6 complex, but it's best to consult your GP or nurse first before taking anything.

Best wishes   *Aunty*

Secret Worries

Dear Aunty

I am really worried about my friend. She has got really thin, she doesn't eat anything and I think she has anorexia. How can I help her?

Lisa, aged 14

Dear Lisa

It's good that you are worried about your friend. Anorexia nervosa is a very serious illness, and if your friend is showing symptoms of this disease, then she must seek help. Try to find out how she feels about herself. If she is anorexic, she will see a really fat girl when she looks in a mirror. No matter how hard you try to convince her she isn't fat, she won't believe you. That is why she eats as little as possible. When she does eat, she feels guilty because she thinks she will get fatter. Ask her about her periods. They may have already stopped. This illness can have tragic results; because some girls starve so much, they get thinner and thinner, and eventually die.

Your friend will most probably tell you she is on a very strict diet. She will also wear baggy clothes so people won't be able to tell how thin she is. She may also take an interest in cooking and preparing her own meals so that she has total control over what she eats. She will pretend she has already eaten a meal, when in reality she has thrown it in the bin. She will eventually stop having periods altogether and will feel cold all the time. This problem is not something you can sort out by yourself. Your friend will need professional help, so she must go to her doctor. You could try ringing one of the helplines for eating disorders at the back of the book for more advice.

Best wishes *Aunty*

Dear Aunty

I have always done really well at school, but just lately I can't concentrate on anything except how I look. Since I started my periods, I seem to be getting fatter and fatter. I just hate it. I have always loved eating and really enjoyed eating out. But now after I have eaten a really delicious meal, and eaten chocolates or cakes, I get really guilty and think how fat I am getting. So I have been making myself sick. I am now doing it at least once a day after I've eaten in the evening, and even more at weekends.
How can I stop?

Grace, aged 13

Dear Grace

It sounds as if you are developing a condition called bulimia (or bulimia nervosa). It is an eating disorder just like anorexia. It is very common in girls like you who worry about their body shape, especially during puberty. You love food, so you eat as much as you like, and then feel really bad about it. You think it will make you fat, so you make yourself sick. Your condition could get worse and you could binge on food, and make yourself sick several times a day. This can lead to lots of medical problems, and your teeth will deteriorate, as the acid in your vomit affects them. It is good that you want to do something about it, because some girls will not face up to the fact that they have a problem. You must talk to an adult about this, or go to your GP straight away. Please look at the back of the book for helplines that will give you more advice.

Best wishes *Aunty*

☆ ☆ ☆ ☆ ☆

Dear Aunty

I'm worried about my sister. I think she has a
drink problem. She's 14 and used to drink just
at weekends but now she's drinking during the
week as well. She says it isn't a problem
because she only drinks lager and she doesn't
always get drunk.

Rachel, aged 11

Dear Rachel

You are right to be worried. Lots of girls
are drinking by the time they are 14. The
occasional drink may not do too much harm,
but if your sister is drinking every day, then it
doesn't sound too good. Drinking a lot of
alcohol is very bad for your health, and can
damage your liver, and at your sister's age, her
liver is not yet fully developed. Please try to
encourage your sister to stop drinking, or at
least try and tell her to cut down, and ask her
why she drinks too much. Maybe she thinks
it's cool – well it isn't. If she is drinking too

much both her brain and body will become badly affected. People often do things they regret when drunk and it could ruin the rest of her life. She could also be reminded that by law she should not be drinking alcohol until she
is 18.

See the back of the book for some useful numbers to call for advice.

Best wishes *Aunty*

☆ ☆ ☆ ☆ ☆

Dear Aunty

I am 14. For some time now I have thought I might be a lesbian. I have dreams about kissing other girls and there is a girl in the year above that I really fancy. I am scared to tell any one about these feelings. What can I do?

Leone, aged 14

Dear Leone

You do need to talk to somebody. Talk to your mum or dad, or if this is difficult you could try telling a teacher you trust. At your age, it's really difficult to know what you really want. Forget about labels and focus on putting your feelings in perspective. A lot of girls your age have crushes on people of the same sex and go on to be heterosexual later.

Your feelings may well change, and it might be some time before you really know what you want. You may decide later that you might be heterosexual, gay or bisexual. Some people do naturally prefer their own sex, and being gay or lesbian is nothing to be ashamed of. If you don't want to talk to somebody you know, look at the helplines, such as the Lesbian and Gay Switchboard, at the back of the book for more advice. You will be able to confide in someone who can relate to your experience, but please don't rush into attaching labels to yourself.

Best wishes *Aunty*

Dear Aunty

I have realised that I am sexually attracted to other girls. I would like to have a proper girl-friend but I don't know what people would say. I want to tell my parents and my friends, but I don't know how. Sometimes I feel as if I am being punished, and I know some of my friends won't want to speak to me any more if I tell them that I'm a lesbian.

Kerrie, aged 14

Dear Kerrie

I know this will be a difficult time for you, but it is good that you are sure about your sexual feelings. You shouldn't worry about your friends. They need to realise that being gay or lesbian is acceptable. Gays and lesbians have equal rights, they have to go to school, go to university or get a job, get ill, just like every-one else. Some people like to pick on gays and lesbians. Well, they shouldn't. They are just being ignorant and there is a lot of nonsense talked about homosexuality. It doesn't really matter what your sexuality is, what colour you are, what religion you are, just as long as you are a good human being.

You will have to make your own decision about when you start telling other people. Some people never 'come out' and it can lead to a life of misery and deceit. Once people come out they find other people aren't so hurtful or curious, and they can lead perfectly happy lives. It will be your decision, and if you can, try and talk to your parents and friends as soon as you feel up to it. However, some parents find their children's sexuality difficult to come to terms with. You might start going to clubs to meet other girls so you can share your experiences about 'coming out' with them. See the helpline at the back of the book for more help.

Best wishes   *Aunty*

☆ ☆ ☆ ☆ ☆

Dear Aunty

My best friend is having a party while her parents are away on holiday, and some girls are
saying they are going to take E (Ecstasy) there,
and that it will be a real laugh. I am 14 and am
really scared to try it. But my friends will think
I am silly if I don't.

What can I do?

Polly, aged 14

Dear Polly

Taking any illegal drug can be dangerous, so
you mustn't feel pressurised into doing something you don't want to do, especially something that is against the law. Don't worry
about your friends; don't let them bully you.
You can say you are not interested in trying
drugs, and you don't need them to have a
good time. Please stick to your guns, because
once you try drugs, you run the risk of getting addicted, being very sick or even dying.

Some people are curious about illegal drugs and want to experiment with them. They think it's cool and that drugs can take your mind off the problems in your life, but it really isn't worth it in the end. Drugs affect your mind, your body, your work, and your life. Keep away from them as they will cause even more problems for you. Some of your friends might not like your attitude, and may already be messing around with drugs. However, a recent survey suggests it is becoming less fashionable to take drugs. Over 70 per cent of 14- to 15-year-olds thought it was unsafe to take Ecstasy or cocaine.

If any of your friends has a drug problem, he or she should contact the National Drugs Helpline listed at the back of the book.

Best wishes   *Aunty*

☆ ☆ ☆ ☆ ☆

Dear Aunty

Recently I had a very big shock. My parents told me that my dad isn't my real dad. My mum had me before she got married, and she has lost all contact with my real dad. My parents have said that I am free to find out more about my real dad if I want to. I can't decide if I want to or not. I don't want to upset my parents, especially my dad, well I think of him as my dad – even now – and I'm not sure I can handle meeting a complete stranger.

Willa, aged 11

Dear Willa

I'm sorry that it gave you such a shock, but it is always difficult for parents to tell their child this kind of news. Your parents have obviously decided that you are mature enough to decide for yourself whether or not you want to seek out your biological father. Some people decide they have no curiosity about their real parents, while others have a deep longing to make contact. There is no hurry for you to come to a decision.

Try to talk to your parents about your confused feelings. If you do want to know more about your biological father, I am sure your parents can give you more information. His name might appear on your birth certificate, and your dad whom you have grown up with, may have adopted you. For more help and advice, look at some of the helplines at the back of the book. The British Agencies of Adoption and Fostering will be able to tell you how you can make contact with your biological father.

Best wishes   *Aunty*

Boys

Dear Aunty

Most of my mates at school already have boyfriends. One of my mates keeps telling me there is a boy in the year above us who fancies me. I can't decide if I'm that interested in him. I'm not sure I want a boyfriend just yet, but my mates keep telling me I should speak to him. Every time I see him, I just get embarrassed and I wouldn't really know what to say to him.

Denise, aged 13

Dear Denise

Don't feel that this boy has to be your boyfriend. It's far better to make friends with him first, before deciding if you want to take things further. Just say 'hello' to him and see what he does next. Act the same around him as you do around girls. You don't have to behave differently. Don't give in to pressure from your mates when it comes to boys. They may be looking for boyfriends all the time, but that doesn't mean you have to – boys can just be friends as well, you know. There's no great rush to start dating. Wait until you feel ready yourself, no matter what your friends are doing. There is enormous pressure on girls these days to grow up very quickly, well, you have the rest of your life for that, so do what you want, not what is expected of you.

Best wishes *Aunty*

☆ ☆ ☆ ☆ ☆

Dear Aunty

There is a boy in the year above me who I really like, and I think he likes me. But I'm too scared to make the first move, and I don't understand why he doesn't say anything to me about it.

Maddie, aged 12

Dear Maddie

Girls find approaching boys very difficult, but boys can find talking to girls just as hard. He is most probably as shy as you are at making the first move. A lot of people hide their feelings because they're scared of rejection. There is no reason why a girl shouldn't approach a boy first. There is no rule that says it always has to be the male who starts things off. Some boys really enjoy it when girls speak first. It means that the girl must like them. The first thing is to make friends with this boy. So try to summon up the courage to speak to him. Once you've made the first move, it won't be so difficult. You can take things easy and see how it goes. Maybe you could go out in a group first. Once you feel relaxed with each other, there may even be romance in the air!

Best wishes   *Aunty*

☆ ☆ ☆ ☆ ☆

Dear Aunty

My friends tell me I'm boy-mad. They say I flirt with every boy I meet. I think I'm just being friendly. What's wrong with that?

Sandy, aged 14

Dear Sandy

A lot of girls go from the stage of hating boys to being almost obsessed by them, i.e. being boy-mad. But this doesn't seem to be so in your case. It's good to be naturally friendly. Maybe your friends are just jealous that you seem to have no trouble chatting and being friendly with the opposite sex, whereas they might be finding it more difficult. Being friendly to boys will help them feel relaxed in your company. However, there are different ways of flirting. Don't say or do anything you're not sure about. Just remember you have to be sincere – you don't have to pretend to be what you're not, or pretend to feel what you don't.

Best wishes   *Aunty*

Dear Aunty

I would really like to have a boyfriend, but there doesn't seem to be anyone around I like. They seem really boring, and I am really interested in lots of different things like the environment. Lots of girls in my class are going out with boys already, but no boy I know seems to be interested in me. I'm not ugly, I get good marks for my schoolwork, so I don't know what the problem is. Help.

Lola, aged 11

Dear Lola

It sounds as if even though you do want a boyfriend, there don't seem to be any boys around who are suitable. Maybe you should make your search wider, and set your goals higher. Rather than waiting to see if any boy you already know might be interested in you, you need to get out and meet a few more boys. Someone who is more on your wavelength. How about joining a sports club, or local youth group? Or if you are interested in the environment or politics for instance, you could join Friends of the Earth, or the youth section of a local political party or action group. I'm sure when you meet someone you like, you'll soon discover whether he likes you or not, and you won't have to hang around much longer. Something will click between you, and if you think he might be a little bit shy, don't worry about making the first move if you have too.

Best wishes   *Aunty*

Sex

Dear Aunty

My friends and I are always talking about sex and what would happen if one of us got pregnant, but I am not really sure about all the facts. Do you always get pregnant if you have sex?

Isla, aged 12

Dear Isla

First of all, it is better if a man and woman have sex only if they really love each other. Unfortunately, however, some girls and boys will get carried away, regardless of their age or even if they are still unsure about their true feelings for each other. You should always make sure that you feel right about having sex. If you have any doubts, then please don't have sex.

A woman must ovulate (produce an egg) to get pregnant, and the man must produce healthy sperm, although a woman does not get pregnant every time she has sex. (See section on periods.) However, regardless of this, it is wise always to use contraception.

When two people have sexual intercourse, or full sex, the man has to put his penis into the woman's vagina. This is called penetrative sex. The man normally has an erection: his penis stiffens and gets hard. When he inserts his penis into a woman's vagina, it feels so good that after a while he will have an orgasm and his sperm will be ejaculated into the woman's vagina. A woman too can feel really good, and she can also reach an orgasm. (But you don't necessarily need to have an orgasm to become pregnant.)

After ejaculation, some of the sperm will travel up inside the woman and one or two of the sperm may meet her egg in one of her fallopian tubes. If the egg is fertilised by the sperm, the egg settles in the woman's uterus (womb) where, in nine months, it gradually grows from an embryo into a full-size baby.

Look at the back of the book for more information. The Brook Advisory Service will be able to give you more details.

Best wishes *Aunty*

☆ ☆ ☆ ☆ ☆

Dear Aunty

I'm 14 and have been going out with a boy for six weeks and he's already trying to touch me down below. He seems to get really heated up, and I'm not sure whether I should stop him or not.

Hattie, aged 14

Dear Hattie

Both boys and girls do get passionate feelings about sex. However, it is really important to develop your relationship with your boyfriend and feel really comfortable with him first. Your boyfriend has to show respect for you and only do things that you are happy about. So even when he is getting really excited, please ask him to slow down if you don't want him touching your genitals. You should only let your boyfriend explore your body when you want him to, and only when you feel ready to explore his body as well.

Best wishes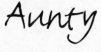

Dear Aunty

One day my boyfriend and I were alone in my house together and we started undressing each other. We both got really excited and started touching each other. Then I changed my mind and wanted to stop. I had never done this kind of thing before and I got scared. Now I am worried I did the wrong thing, and upset him by not carrying on. Was I right or wrong to stop?

Delia, aged 14

Dear Delia

At the moment you and your boyfriend are still getting to know each other. With time and when you feel safe in your relationship, you might want to explore each other's body more and more. You might even stimulate each other's sexual organs (called mutual masturbation), but again, only do this if you feel absolutely ready. If you feel the slightest bit uncomfortable about any sexual activity, tell your boyfriend. He should only do what you want him to do. He shouldn't get upset at you if you don't want to carry on. If he ignores you, then he is being selfish and is not worth knowing. So, yes, you were right to stop.

The other thing is that sometimes you do get carried away, and then it is too late to stop. You could end up having unprotected sex. And, if you ever do decide to have sex, always insist that your boyfriend wears a condom. If he hasn't got one, or you haven't got one, then please forget the whole thing. And one more thing, remember that until the age of 16 sex is illegal.

Best wishes   *Aunty*

Dear Aunty

My ex-boyfriend has been telling all his mates that I'm rubbish in bed, but this is ridiculous, because we never had sex. I am still a virgin and plan to stay that way until I'm older. I'm pretty sure he's still a virgin too, although he was keen for me to go the whole way with him. I don't understand – why is he lying about me?

Gina, aged 14

Dear Gina

Some boys do lie about having sex when they haven't. They feel they have to boast to their mates about it, when sometimes they're just as scared as girls about the whole thing. Your ex might be blaming you for the fact you didn't go the whole way with him, and is lying about you to get his own back. Basically he's just trying to make up for his own inadequacies, so ignore what he's saying. He obviously isn't worth it, and thank goodness he is no longer your boyfriend. It's good to stand up for your principles and keep your virginity. Nobody should push you into having sex, when you're not ready. When you find the right person, you will know when it's right. Hopefully your ex-boyfriend will realise this one day too.

Best wishes *Aunty*

☆ ☆ ☆ ☆ ☆

Dear Aunty

My best friend says you should never have sex with a boy because you can get a disease. What does she mean?

Henrietta, aged 11

Dear Henrietta

Your friend is being rather dramatic. But yes, it is possible that having sex may give you a disease. Before any girl has sex with the boy she loves, she must make sure she knows him really well, and that he has no infection that can be passed on by sex. Every time a girl does have sex she should ensure her partner wears a condom. This helps to stop pregnancy, but is also a protection against sexual infections. There are various kinds of sexual infections, such as HIV, AIDS, gonorrhoea, and herpes. They are called Sexually Transmitted Diseases or STDs for short. If you know of anyone who may have an infection of this kind then tell them to contact the Brook Advisory Helpline for further advice and information.

Best wishes *Aunty*

Helplines

Accept Services – Telephone 020 7371 7477 for counselling about drinking.

Alateen – Telephone 020 7403 0888 for advice about alcoholics.

Anti-Bullying Campaign –
Telephone 020 7378 1446 for counselling and advice about bullying.

The British Agencies of Adoption and Fostering – Telephone 020 7593 2000 for information and advice for adopted or fostered children.

British Association for Counselling –
Telephone 01788 550899 for local counsellors.

Brook Advisory Helpline – Freephone 0800 018 5023 any time for information about contraception, pregnancy, abortion, STDs, emergency contraception.

Careline – Telephone 020 8514 1177.
Counselling and advice on any problem.

Centre for Eating Disorders –
National Helpline 020 8959 2330.

ChildLine – Freephone 0800 1111 any time.
Confidential advice for young people on any
problem.

Cruse Bereavement Care – Telephone 0345
585565 for counselling for the bereaved.

Drinkline – Freephone 0800 9178282 confidential information and advice for anyone with a
drink problem or anyone concerned about someone with a drink problem.

Eating Disorders Association – Telephone
01603 765050. Both offer support for people suf-
fering from anorexia, bulimia, compulsive eating
or those with weight worries.

Family Planning Association England –
Telephone 020 7837 4044 for advice on sex-
related issues and information on nearest clinics.

Family Planning Association Northern Ireland – Telephone 02890 325488.

Family Planning Association Scotland – Telephone 0141 576 5088.

Family Planning Association Wales – Telephone 0845 6001213.

Health Information Service – Freephone 0800 66 55 44 for information on various health issues.

Lesbian and Gay Switchboard – Telephone 020 7837 7324 for information and advice on being gay, lesbian or bisexual.

Muslim Women's Helpline – Telephone 020 8904 8193 or 020 8908 6715. Advice and support for Muslim women.

National AIDS Helpline – Freephone 0800 567123 any time for confidential advice on HIV and AIDS.

National Child Protection – Freephone 0800 800500.

National Drugs Helpline – Freephone 0800 776600 for 24-hour advice.

Parentline – Telephone 0808 8002222 to talk through any issues about parents.

Quitline – Freephone 0800 002200 for help and counselling for smokers, plus free information pack on how to stop smoking.

Rape Crisis Centre – Telephone 020 7837 1600 for confidential counselling about rape or assault.

Relate – Telephone 01788 573241 for counselling about relationships.

Release – Telephone 020 7729 9904 for advice on drugs.

The Samaritans – Telephone 08457 909090 any time.

Sexwise – Freephone 0800 282930 to talk to an adviser about sex and personal relationships.

Talk Adoption – Freephone 0800 7831234 for those involved in adoption.

Women's Aid National Helpline – Telephone 08457 023468 to find local support.

Youth Access – Telephone 020 8772 9900. Details on where to locate counselling and advisory services locally.

Educational Information

BBC Pack – Key Stage 3 – Telephone 08456 101533 for more information.

www.anglia.co.uk/deducatin/mathsnet/ – Maths resources, games and puzzles.

www.bbc.co.uk/education/gcsebitesize – Revision guide for GCSE.

www.bbc.co.uk/knowledge/bitesistc-maths2.shtml – GCSE maths revision.

www.booktrust.org.uk – Information on educational books.

www.education.co.uk/learning – Guardian educational website.

www.enchantedlearning.com – Educational activities.

www.gcse.com/recep.htm – GCSE answers, an idea of what examiners are looking for, syllabus details, tips for revising for pupils who need to build their confidence.

www.gcseworld.cjb.net – GCSE information.

www.homeworkhigh.com – Channel 4's kids learning site.

www.4learning.co.uk/firs-edition – Channel 4 current affairs First Edition Quiz on subjects such as sex education.

www.ukonline.co.uk/webwise/spinneret/ – GCSE biology.

www.ulen.com/shakespeare/ – Website about studying Shakespeare.

Websites –
General Information

www.bbc.co.uk/health/kids – Body and mind matters.

www. bodyform.co.uk – Information on sanitary towels.

www.childline.org.uk – ChildLine's website including clear and accessible information on bullying, eating problems, abuse, racism and bereavement. Plus a message board called Get Talking where you can chat to other people about various problems.

www.drugsinfofile.com – Information about the dangers of drugs, hard facts, practical advice and signs to look for.

www.Learnfree.co.uk – For information about education.

www.relate.org.uk – Relate website.

www.SafeKids.com and
www.SafeTeens.com – Advice list for children and teenagers about using the net safely. How to contact educational and other sites of interest.

www.samaritans.org – Deals with issues young people are concerned about.

www.tacade.com – Lifeskills, health, alcohol and drugs information.

www.tampax.com – For any questions about tampons.

www.trashed.co.uk – The Health Education Authority's drug information site.

For information on sanitary protection write to:
Always, PO Box 1030, Llangollen, Clwyd, LL20 8YW.